This book was devised and produced by
Multimedia Publications (UK) Ltd

Editor: Richard Rosenfeld
Production: Arnon Orbach
Design: John Strange
Picture Research: Helena Beaufoy,
Catherine Blackie

First published 1984 by Octopus Books
Limited, 59 Grosvenor Street, Lonon W 1

ISBN 0-7064-2251-1

Color origination by D. S. Colour International
Ltd, London. Printed in Spain by Cayfosa,
Barcelona Dep. Leg. B-21733

BOY GEORGE
& CULTURECLUB

BOY GEORGE & CULTURECLUB

Introduction

IT IS A SUNNY DAY IN MIDTOWN MANHATTAN. The cars and cabs on Fifth Avenue drone past the bustle of sober-suited businessmen and secretaries out to grab a quick lunch.

Suddenly the crowds and the traffic stop as a figure emerges from a hotel doorway. It is decked out in a rabbi's hat, crowning plaits and ribbons, and a brightly patterned dress covered in strange symbols dominated by the Star of David. The face is made up to its perfectly penciled arched eyebrows. Passers-by gasp in amazement. Everyone is staring wide-eyed as the multicolored vision parades past.

Outrageous style

Since that day the whole country – in fact the whole world – has gone crazy about Boy George in one way or another. Confused press and parents have condemned his outrageous style, while fans have flocked to buy his records, attend his concerts and dress like him.

Boy George is the first real pop superstar of the eighties. Clever, quick and colorful, he has charmed and alarmed millions with his bizarre dress and exotic music.

At first he was seen as a threat to the nation's morals. One eminent Los Angeles newspaper even went so far as to advise worried parents to lock up their daughters *and* their sons because of the gigantic, incoming wave of British transvestites.

No one was sure if Boy George was really a boy or a girl. The American-based International Bachelor Women's Society was an exception. Its members had no doubts on the subject whatsoever. In 1984 they voted him one of the world's 10 most desirable bachelors.

"Drag queen"

Boy George and his dazzling band Culture Club have had records in the charts continuously since the end of 1982 when they hit the top with *Do You Really Want To Hurt Me?* All six singles they've released have reached the Top 10 and, in 1984, they won the coveted Grammy Award for Best New Artist.

The same year they smashed the Number One spot with *Karma Chameleon.* And in typical fashion Boy George thanked America by joking, "You've got good taste, style and you know a good drag queen when you see one."

Boy George has been accused of everything. Of corrupting the nation's youth. Of being an overmade-up hype. Of being bitchy. Yet few who have met him have failed to be charmed by his intelligence, humor and kindness.

When he visited one American town a fan wrote and invited him to dinner. George was too busy on that occasion to accept but still found the time next time round to send her a taped message with his thanks. And, most importantly, few who have heard his records or seen him on stage have failed to be impressed by his singing and his talent.

But who is he? Who is this Boy George who has stormed the charts and hearts of the world, disturbing and delighting everyone of every age, leaving them reeling in his perfumed wake?

He was born plain George Alan O'Dowd on June 14, 1961 to working class Irish Catholic parents in the south-east London area of Woolwich, where he grew up with four brothers and a sister. His father, Jeremiah, was a builder. The family, always a close-knit one, was pretty poor in those early days.

Expelled

In his spare time, George's father ran a boxing club and, when George was younger, he used to work out on the punch bags. He hasn't really stopped fighting since.

Always the rebel, George hated the rules and rigors of school. The other boys ridiculed him because he couldn't play soccer and, later, because of his high voice and exotic clothes. "I always preferred to hang out with girls rather than boys," says George. "Girls tend to be more innocent than boys – and also prettier. I felt that I had more in common with them. And you can make of that what you like."

Life became harder for the young George as he grew up realizing he was an individual and would have to develop his own character if he was going to survive. He started dyeing his hair bright orange – imitating his then hero David Bowie – which caused great problems at school.

George had gained a reputation for being one of the most unruly pupils. He and the principal of his school in south London clashed – often violently. Much of the time George played truant but when he did attend he found himself dumped in a special room with all the other "unteachables" under the watchful eye of a psychiatrist.

"I didn't get on very well at school," George admits. "I'm the sort of person who picks up things and then drops them. The sort of suburban school I went to tried to take away my identity. I wanted to do English and Art but I had to do all the other stuff as well."

The crunch came when – after an enormous row with the principal over taking time off and refusing to be caned – George was expelled in 1976 at the age of 15.

Glamor and abuse

His father wanted him to join the family building business, which was by then doing well, but George knew it was not for him. He wanted other things in life.

George's passion for dressing up in gaudy and outrageous outfits also caused trouble at home. There were rows and tensions. "When I first started experimenting with different colors and clothes, my mother tried to keep me indoors," George recalls.

This was the time in Britain directly after the glitter rock craze started by groups such as T-Rex, and just before the hard core punk revolution which turned sounds, styles and attitudes completely upside down. Even the youth cults – always renowned for being at the sharp end of any fashion craze – were completely in the doldrums.

Flared jeans, long hair and pointed collars were the order of the day. So George's over-the-top struttings caused much attention and, in some quarters, abuse. Luckily for George, he found a group of like-minded people to run around with and together they descended on the gay clubs of London – the only places where they knew that they could avoid getting beaten up for the way they chose to dress.

Then just as punk was beginning to make its influence felt, George started to visit shops in Chelsea's King's Road searching out some even wilder ideas.

Suddenly, the whole pop music scene exploded into life — and nothing was ever to be the same again.

Simon Tebbutt
London 1984

Chapter 1
Rebel Superstar

After leaving school, George found life at home stifling and eventually moved to stay with friends in Birmingham and London. Here he really discovered himself, working in clothes' shops and as a make-up artist for the Royal Shakespeare Company. He also did some modeling and appeared in a string of advertisements. He was a punk looking skyward in a TV advertisement for British Airways. Now he seems to spend more time flying around the world than on the ground.

Life in the squats
George, with his wild make up and clothes, soon became a "face" on the crazy London club scene of the late seventies. He moved into the famous squats – illegally occupied houses – in Warren Street and Carburton Street and soon learned to live by his wits, defending himself with his sharp tongue.

Life in the squats was an endless fancy dress party. All the freaks, artists, fashion designers and photographers, dressed and painted like weird characters from a horror movie, flocked to the squats for days of riotous fun.

Cover star
In 1978 George's crowd started their own club, The Blitz, in London's Covent Garden. The Blitz quickly became the launching pad for the sharp "futurist" and elaborate "new Romantic" movements that were sweeping the British pop scene, spawning groups like Duran Duran and Spandau Ballet. London's young people were tired of dressing like extras from *Saturday Night Fever* and latched onto the craze with fevered enthusiasm.

They began dressing to the hilt in frills and finery in a never-ending attempt to outdo each other. Dull dressers were refused admission. Only the outrageous were admitted.

Magazine photographers massed to catch the strange goings on. George was one of the most photographed faces and appeared on covers all over the world, shocking everyone who caught sight of him.

But he realized he was just drifting. "It was all so shallow," he says now. "I wanted to do something more valuable."

So, with a few friends, George started a futurist band with the odd name In Praise Of Lemmings. Then one night at Planets he drunkenly approached Malcolm McLaren – the man behind the Sex Pistols who was then managing Bow Wow Wow – to tell him he wanted to sing. This led to his short-lived career as Lieutenant Lush, playing with Bow Wow Wow and stealing the show at London's Rainbow Theatre. George now decided it was time to sharpen up his image and form his own band.

Top: Only a handful of people had any idea who Boy George was when he first toured America in the mirror shades and white cap. Now, with his sensational shows and music, everyone knows Boy George. He has sold so many millions of records that he can even afford to have shirts made, jokingly littered with dollar signs (*above*).

Below: George has a radical and sharp eye for make-up ideas and has been practicing with cosmetics since he was at school. But he only paints his face because he thinks it makes him look better. George's idea of real beauty has more to do with the person than the image and he admits his physical faults. He argues that it is still possible to be attractive with an imperfect body.

Even when Boy George and Culture Club released the chart-topping, smash hit *Do You Really Want To Hurt Me?*, few had any idea what superstars they would become, least of all the music reviewers. "Third time lucky for George and the boys? Don't think so, this is weak, watered down fourth division reggae. Awful." wrote one pop critic. Another reviewer wrote, "It's plain that the group's only asset is the ludicrously unphotogenic Boy George. God help 'em." Within weeks, Culture Club had rocketed to the top in Britain and followed up their success in almost every other country.

Boy George is now a critically acclaimed singer, loved by his millions of fans all over the world. But he got his first break on stage merely as a stand-in for Bow Wow Wow's Annabella. She was giving manager Malcolm McLaren such problems that he decided temporarily to replace her to bring her back into line. George, needless to say, stole the show, held at London's Rainbow Theatre in 1981. McLaren's trick worked so well that Annabella agreed to become the kind of pop star he wanted her to be. George was dumped!

Almost singlehandedly, Boy George has been responsible for revolutionizing the British fashion industry. British designers are now respected all over the world and have stolen the limelight from former fashion centers in New York, Paris and Milan. It is amazing to think that George first developed his stunning looks by dressing very cheaply in cast-offs bought from secondhand stores. George is living proof that people do not need to have a lot of money to look stylish. All you need is good taste – and George's confidence!

In every country that Boy George visits these days he is confronted with lookalike images of himself. Not since the days of the Beatles have people imitated a style so slavishly. His look received the blessing of respectability when London's waxworks museum Madame Tussauds – where all the top movie stars and politicians are frozen in time – decided to include Boy George in their hallowed ranks.

Only three other rock stars are on show there, Elton John, Elvis Presley and David Bowie. "We took the Beatles out some time ago because we thought they'd become rather dated," says a spokesman for the museum. "And there's no chance of us including Duran Duran. They're simply not in Boy George's league."

Center: Boy George and his Japanese friend Miko at the French airport where he was nearly refused admission to the country. When reporters saw the pair together the papers were full of stories that they were lovers. In fact, they have been very good friends for a long time. George says that he loves all his friends, although not necessarily in a sexual way.

Chapter 2
King of Fashion

Today Boy George is as famous for his astonishing clothes and make-up as he is for his music. He is a born poseur, born for the cameras, a walking pin-up come true for millions.

Everyone on the London nightclub scene remembers George – they could hardly forget someone who regularly painted his face green, or red, even purple – but no one guessed what a star he would be. George knew better. "I decided to look more outrageous than anyone with the make-up and dresses," he says.

"Gender bender"
George looked so amazing when he burst on to the British pop scene in 1981 that *everyone* took notice. It didn't matter if they roared loudly. George knew he would have the last laugh. The press screamed he was a "gender bender". Now they're queuing for fashion features and running lookalike competitions.

His image is deliberately confusing. George's style usually comes out tops and he is often voted the best male *and* the best female singer in polls, though he was called one of the worst dressed women in the world by famous Los Angeles designer Mr. Blackwell.

Although he has dressed in all fashions from an early age, the special Boy George look came about when he was working as a window dresser in a store in London's Covent Garden. Here he bumped into the adventurous designer Sue Clowes who was working in large prints, tribal insignia, gypsy symbols and Jewish signs. The pair set up another shop round the corner, called The Foundry. With Boy George's rasta dreadlocks and rabbi hat, the distinctive Culture Club image was born and rapidly became famous.

"I wear Y-fronts"
"Everything had to be made extra large for George," Sue says. "He wouldn't have short sleeves because he's got short, fat, hairy arms. And dresses had to be made to suit his figure, so they didn't make his bum look too big or whatever. And the prints had to be made brighter for him."

George's clothes are now all made for him by designer Dexter Wong.

George is very sure that when it comes to fashion he has got it right. "I'm not a transvestite," he declares. "I wear Y-fronts. I'm a man, I wear make-up and dress like this because I think it makes me look better.

"But despite what people probably imagine, I don't believe in clothes. I don't believe you should believe in what you wear. That's a silly philosophy and not much to base a life on."

Far left: Do you really want to hurt me? Boy George in a pensive mood, perhaps recalling the hard times before he made it to the top.

Below: Boy George is always in his element on stage. He is a natural performer.

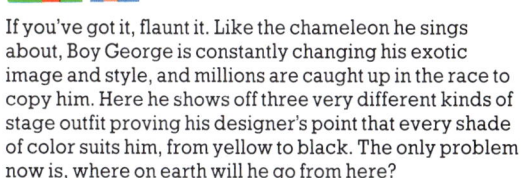

If you've got it, flaunt it. Like the chameleon he sings about, Boy George is constantly changing his exotic image and style, and millions are caught up in the race to copy him. Here he shows off three very different kinds of stage outfit proving his designer's point that every shade of color suits him, from yellow to black. The only problem now is, where on earth will he go from here?

Many people find it hard to believe that Boy George has actually toned down his look over the years. An early shot from his crazy nightclub days when he was the flashiest dresser in town shows him in his Marlene Dietrich mode (*far left*). Now George is *Kissing To Be Clever* and playing at being coy George (*below*). Here he's in subdued pink, sporting the special peak that his fans love to wear at Culture Club concerts.

Although Boy George firmly maintains that he is a man and not a transvestite, he does admit to having a very feminine side. "I think I look like Rita Hayworth here," he says of this perfectly posed shot (*far right*). One of George's favorite hobbies is collecting dolls and toys (*right*). His fans, in turn, collect doll-like images of him. But when he takes to the stage, George shows just how aggressive he really can be (*below*), holding everyone spellbound.

George's passion for make-up (*far right*) has often landed him in trouble. Coming through London Airport (*right*) George was delayed for hours by customs men who forced him to pay duty on gifts bought in America. "It's disgusting. All the money we bring into this country," George snorted. It was even worse in France when immigration officials held him up for five hours, refusing to believe he was a man, arguing that transvestites were banned!

Even when casually dressed, Boy
George is always perfectly made up
(*right*). At other times, however, his
outfits nearly cause riots. And not just
because his clothes are so outrageous.
Rastas were infuriated with his
dreadlocks and Jews objected to the use
of Hebrew insignia on his shirt (*far right*).
But George claims he is trying to bring
people from different cultures together
which is why he donned the Yankee
Doodle Dandy look (*above right*). On
one of Culture Club's American tours
they mixed the American Stars and
Stripes with the British Union Jack flag as
a gesture of friendliness.

Chapter 3
Culture Club

When Boy George first started his band Culture Club in 1981 he wrote to a television pop program asking for an appearance. They turned him down as unsuitable. Three years later Culture Club were so busy conquering the world they had to turn down Prince Charles' request for them to appear at a Royal Variety performance – usually the peak of any performer's career.

Magical ingredients

Boy George is such a larger-than-life character that people often forget the other three members of Culture Club. The most experienced musician in the band is drummer Jon Moss, 27, from north London. Jon worked as a salesman, a printer and a van driver before joining up with local bands and playing brief spells with punk heroes the Clash and the Damned. A bad car crash in 1977 put him out of action for a while. Then one day the phone rang – it was George who had obtained the number from a friend. Fate was smiling that day. Jon's business brain and ear for a good commercial tune coupled with George's flamboyance and imagination were the magical ingredients that were to bring success.

Guitarist Roy Hay was brought up in Basildon, Essex. School was followed by a couple of fruitless jobs. In 1981 he joined a group called Russian Bouquet. Then, quite simply, a friend bumped into George one day and discovered he was looking for a guitarist.

Mikey Craig, 24, is the only black member of the band. Born in Hammersmith, London, he hit the London music scene pretty early on working as a DJ and then in a studio. When he heard George was putting a band together he asked a friend to introduce him – and he was in, as bass guitarist.

Culture Club practiced and practiced, found they had a magic and the first songs were written.

Smash hit

The band recorded a couple of tracks for EMI Records but eventually – after picking up manager Tony Gordon and a few small shows around the country – they signed with Virgin. Two singles *White Boy* and *I'm Afraid Of Me* brought them a little fame and, because of George's looks, more than a little notoriety.

Then they teamed up with producer Steve Levine and recorded two tracks *I'll Tumble* and *Do You Really Want To Hurt Me?* Luckily, they chose the latter for their next single. Inside a month it hit the Number One spot in Britain.

The rest is, as they say, history. Every single has been a smash hit. Their two albums *Kissing To Be Clever* and *Colour By Numbers* have been best sellers and in 1984 Culture Club played their tumultuous sell-out United States tour.

Previous pages: Meet Jon Moss, Boy George, of course, Mikey Craig and Roy Hay, *l. to r.*

"The band comes first," says Culture Club's bass player Mikey Craig. "You have to make yourself lonely. We keep our private lives – especially women – at bay. I had a girlfriend last year who went to America when the band took off. She knew it would finish our relationship. But Roy's just got married. He's hardly seen his wife, Alison. It's hard to take the separation."

Boy George and Culture Club (*below* and *previous pages*) have picked up dazzling awards all over the world. Here, George receives the *Daily Mirror* Readers' Award (*bottom right*) for Outstanding Music Personality in 1982. A year later he was at another occasion (*right*), again stealing the limelight.

Overleaf: Culture Club with designer Sue Clowes and her friend Cass, standing left of Boy George.

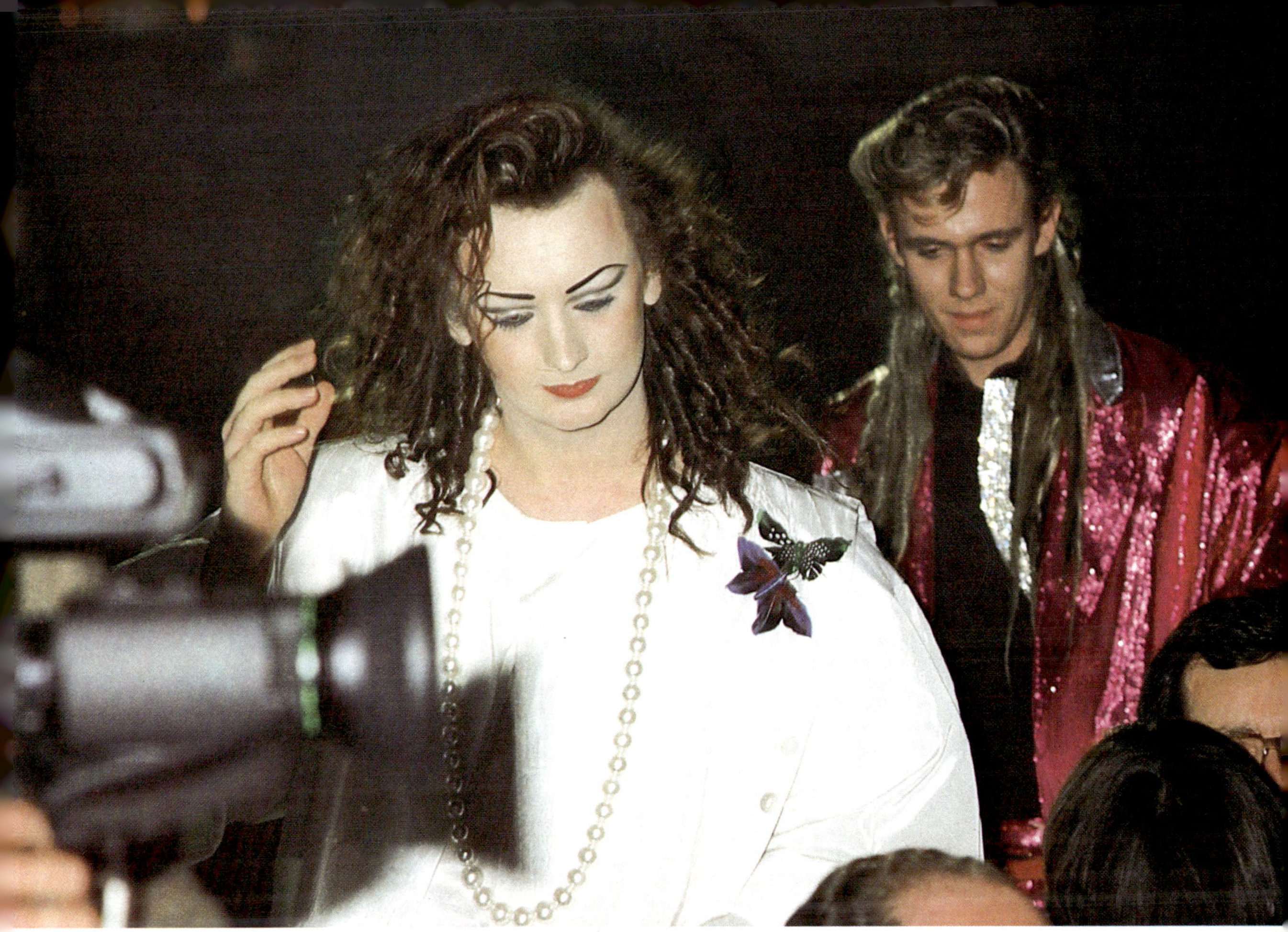

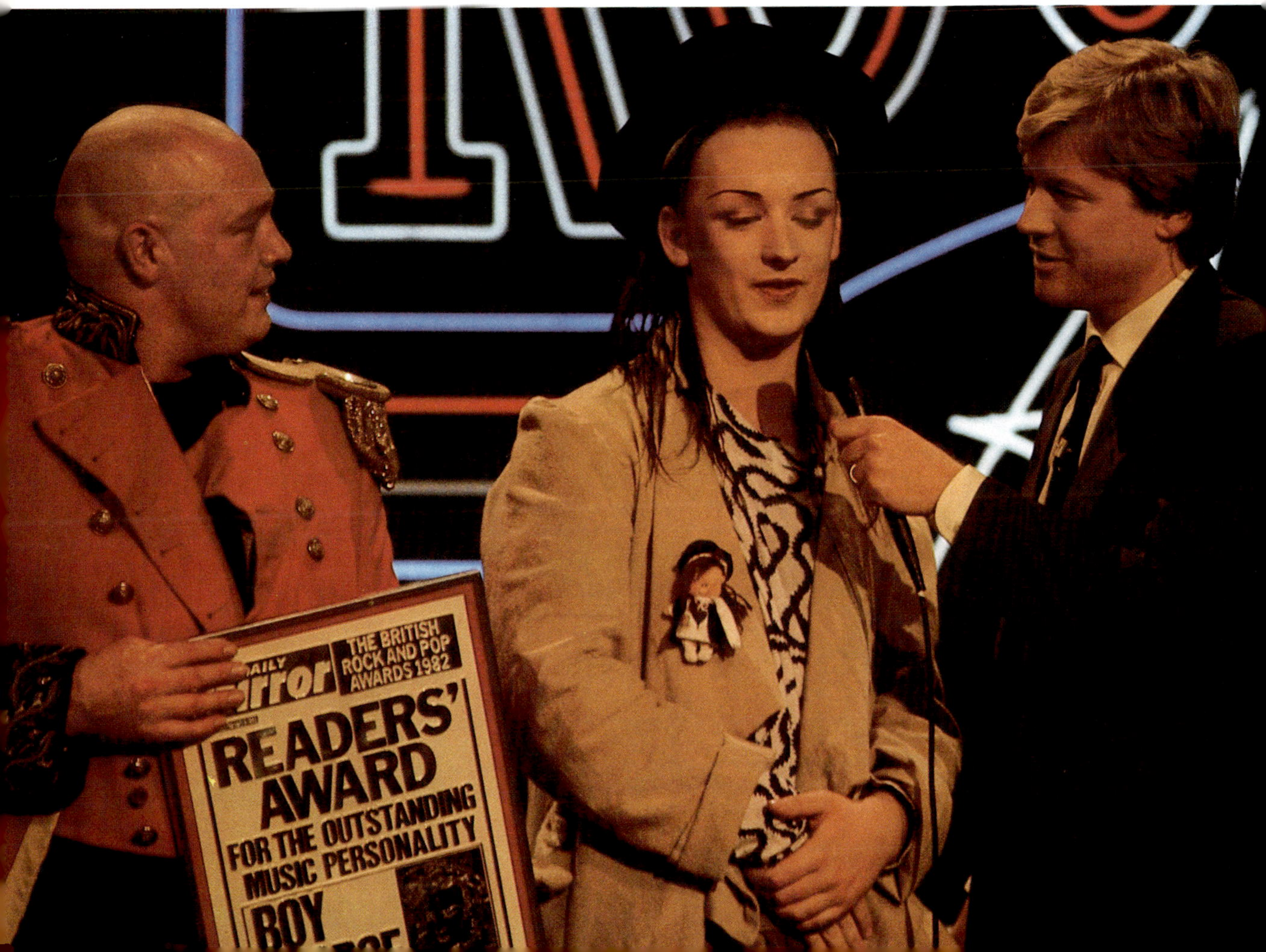
THE BRITISH ROCK AND POP AWARDS 1982
READERS' AWARD
FOR THE OUTSTANDING MUSIC PERSONALITY
BOY

Despite his central position in the group, Boy George never forgets that Culture Club (*below* and *overleaf*) *is* a band and that he owes his success to them. "But I didn't want musos," says George. "I wanted people who hadn't been in bands before. It's not the clever little pop package people seem to think it is."

Right: George receiving an award for the kind of sound and performance that have made Culture Club enormously popular the world over. From the early days, the band set out to reach as many people as possible with their music and not just aim for the fashion-conscious trendies.

Left: Before he heard himself in the studio, Boy George was not really sure of his voice and used to try to copy other singers. "Now I think I've got a good voice," he says. "I'm really pleased with it. If I'd felt in the studio that it wasn't good enough, I'd have given up there and then."

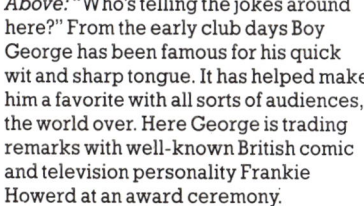

Above: "Who's telling the jokes around here?" From the early club days Boy George has been famous for his quick wit and sharp tongue. It has helped make him a favorite with all sorts of audiences, the world over. Here George is trading remarks with well-known British comic and television personality Frankie Howerd at an award ceremony.

Below: Guess who is hogging the limelight, as usual? Jon Moss (second from the left) casts a glance offstage as the spotlight falls on Boy George. However, there are no tensions in Culture Club, even though everyone wants to focus their lenses and thoughts on George. The group share all the musical decisions equally and, more importantly, split the money four ways. The others simply accept that Boy George has a strange superstar charisma and are happy to get on with making the music.

Top right and *right:* "You know the words, I'll hum along." Boy George on stage with Culture Club and Helen Terry. Helen's majestic voice has added weight and sparkle to the band's sound ever since George asked her to join them for the single *Church Of The Poison Mind*. A professional singer for some ten years – she sang on Lou Reed's classic *Walk On The Wild Side* – Helen is a firm favorite on stage.

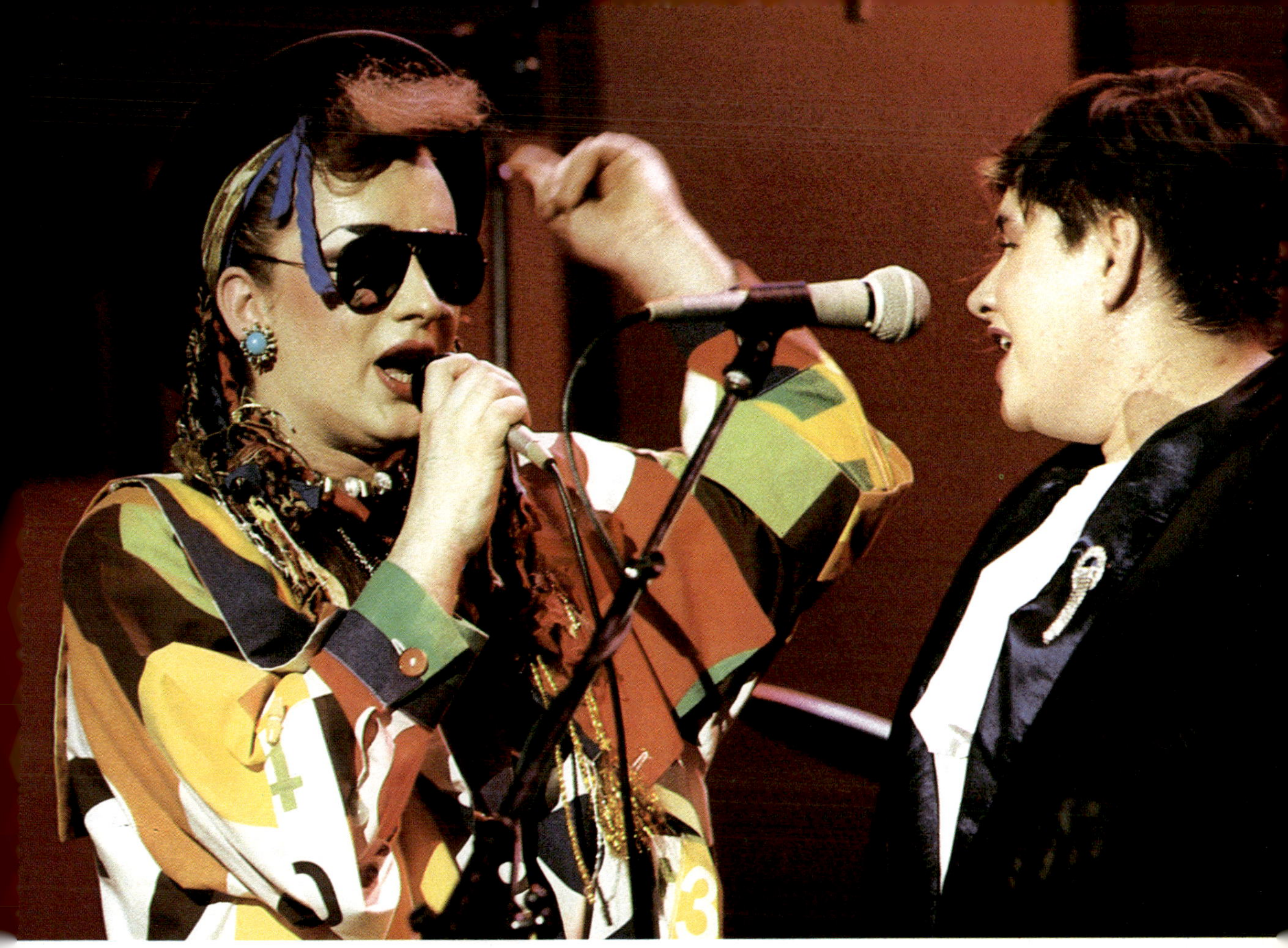

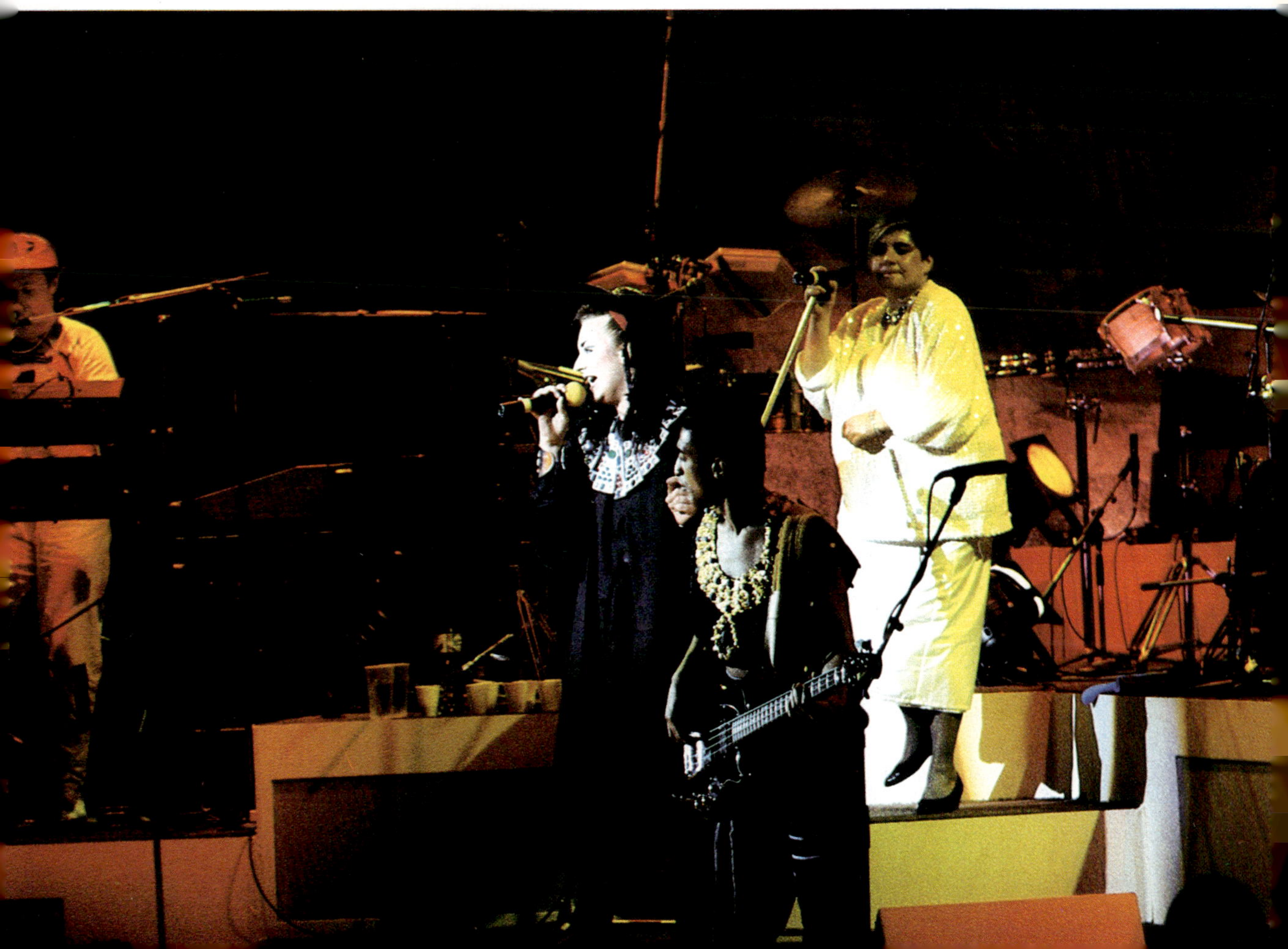

Chapter 4
George, Sex & Fame

Even when he is not performing, Boy George is drawing stares, comments and crowds. And he is always ready with an answer whether serious or funny. Boy George's offstage remarks are as revealing as any of his songs. Disarming, witty and honest he is one of the brightest pop stars.

Boy George on Sex:
"I could get anyone I want, but I prefer a cup of tea to sex ... I don't think to myself that I must go out to a club and find someone to sleep with."

"I've been in love with lots of boys and girls but right now there's no one in my life. I'm too busy working."

Boy George on Boy George:
"I'm a poof with muscles, but under all these clothes and make-up I am a very ordinary person."

"I wasn't born with any special magic. Sometimes I've got a spotty skin, or I feel sick."

Boy George on fame:
"I don't want to end up being a three-minute wonder. I'd rather wait for what I'm going to get ... if I'm going to get it."

"I don't want to be a boring pop star. I don't want to be a rock star and I never will ..."

Boy George on religion:
"I believe in Karma. What you do in this world always comes back to you. I used to do vile things to people and I always got hurt back. I used to be a thief taking things that didn't belong to me, until someone I loved had everything nicked and I realized how vile I was being. I've grown up a lot since then."

Boy George on drugs:
"If someone is smoking a joint I go out of the room. That kind of behavior is a bit passé after all."

Boy George on his songs:
"My life and the way I feel is important to my music because I write about how I feel and about the people I know."

"Most of my songs are very personal and are cynical love songs. Not because I've been unlucky in love, but because it's easier to write sad songs."

Boy George on love:
"I fall in love all the time ... I think people should fall in love a lot. It's great. Wonderful ..."

Boy George on being bitchy:
"I am bitchy, but I'm not a bitch for the sake of being bitchy. I'm not nasty. I don't think so anyway."

Previous pages: "No, he's taking the photograph of *me*." George and painted friend vie for attention in an early club shot.

Right and *below right:* When George first started experimenting with clothes and make-up his mother used to try and keep him in. Now she enjoys dressing up like him (*below*). "Old ladies ask me, 'Is 'e your son? I wouldn't have him in the house'," says Mrs. Diana O'Dowd, George's mother. "But that's only because they don't know him . . ."

Far right: Londoners are constantly amazed to see Boy George cycling around the city. But by the time they have realized it was him he has disappeared!

Right: George in sultry mood, with Roy Hay behind, and (*below*) turning it on for the press.

Previous pages: The public and private faces of Boy George.

Chapter 5
What They Say

It is the test of a true star when people start talking about them. And it seems the whole world is talking about Boy George.

"Non." French immigration official refusing Boy George entry to the country. They fought for five hours before the officials gave in.

"He has always been such a loving son. He phones me every day …" Diana O'Dowd, George's mother.

"He'd throw jealous dramas over trivial things like if someone nicked his make-up ideas or talked to someone he fancied." Ex-nightclub friend.

"George O'Dowd was a classic example of the word misfit. He did not fit in and he did not want to … He did not like the fact that you had to behave and work … He did not get on well with his teachers nor with the other boys and girls." Boy George's ex-principal.

"I think he's got a great voice." Jermaine Jackson.

"He is my son and I love him as much as I love my five other children. He is a lot tougher than he appears to be from the clothes and make-up. If George belted you, you'd know about it." Jeremiah O'Dowd, George's father.

"George was never the cleanest of people. He'd go to great efforts to get made-up and dressed up but he rarely washed. His skin looked revolting without make up." An ex-nightclub friend.

"He dresses like a faggot … but I'm gonna adopt him. Young Kerry, my 18-year-old granddaughter, is in love with him. He's one helluva character … but I can't say I've heard his music." Movie Star Robert Mitchum.

"We've been used to George dressing up and showing off since he was a little kid." George's older brother Richard.

"I was asked what the average Australian would think of George, and I said they'd probably think he's a bloody pooftah. But then I thought, the average Australian probably doesn't even realize he's a man." Greg Ham, Men At Work.

"A lot of people have said 'what a weirdo' and I'm glad to have proved them wrong. George is a very normal bloke really – just a little on the neurotic side." Jon Moss, Culture Club.

"He sings off key. He is consistently flat and I can't stand listening to him." Darryl Hall from duo Hall and Oates.

Left and *right:* When George takes to the stage, no expense is spared. Note the glittering earrings and, as usual, the immaculately applied make up.

Some people still feel threatened by Boy George's over-the-top dress style and exquisitely applied make-up. To them he is a vamp, a monster and a transvestite. But underneath all the finery, George is really just an ordinary human being with sensible attitudes and a strong moral code. Being a pop star, there are plenty of people who offer to go to bed with him. George finds this whole scene sickening and is far more interested in emotional relationships than sexual athletics.

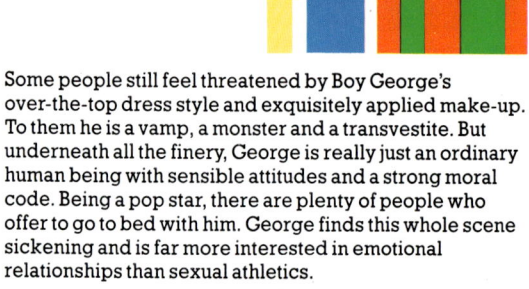

Below: Away from the spotlight, George enjoys a more intimate moment sharing a cup of tea at London's Savoy Hotel with new friend and one of America's funniest ladies, Joan Rivers. Joan is just one of a startling array of stars to fall under George's spell. The pair share the same savage wit. She interviewed him in the *Tonight* television show and asked him what he liked to do in bed. "Sleep," replied George. Joan has been captivated ever since and the pair meet up whenever they can.

Left: George has been photographed so many times and his look copied by so many people everywhere that it is hard to imagine the shock that pictures like this first caused when they were shown in America. Reporters were sent over to Britain to investigate the 'transvestite' craze.

They filed back their copy claiming that worried mothers and fathers were panicking and seeing George almost as the end of civilization. A slight exaggeration but even in Britain – which has a far stronger tradition for wildly dressed eccentrics – more than a few eyebrows were raised when George first strolled around London streets dressed like this (*below*). With typical English reserve, the majority of people ignored him or hurried by. But, as always, there were those who would shout out abuse. What they didn't realize was that George actually enjoyed the attention.

Boy George and Jon Moss collect
another one of the glittering prizes
heaped on Culture Club's head. Not
since the heady days of the swinging
sixties, and the Beatles and the Rolling
Stones, has a pop group caused so much
excitement among so many people
around the globe.

Discography

7 INCH SINGLES

A. *Do You Really Want To Hurt Me?*
B. *You Know I'm Not Crazy*

A. *Time (Clock Of The Heart)*
B. *Romance Beyond The Alphabet*
   (Time Instrumental)

A. *I'll Tumble 4 Ya*
B. *Mystery Boys*

A. *Church Of The Poison Mind*
B. *Mystery Boys*

A. *Karma Chameleon*
B. *That's The Way*

A. *Miss Me Blind*
B. *Color By Numbers*

A. *It's A Miracle*
B. *Love Twist*

12 INCH SINGLES

A. *I'll Tumble 4 Ya*
B. *Man Shake*

A. *It's A Miracle*
B. *Love Twist*

A. *Miss Me Blind*
B. *Color By Numbers*

A. *It's A Miracle* (Dance Remix)
B. *Color By Numbers*

ALBUMS

Kissing To Be Clever
A. *Do You Really Want To Hurt Me?, I'm Afraid Of Me, You Know I'm Not Crazy, I'll Tumble 4 Ya, Love Twist.*
B. *Time (Clock Of The Heart), Boy Boy (I'm The Boy), White Boys Can't Control It, Take Control.*

Color By Numbers
A. *Karma Chameleon, It's A Miracle, Black Money, Changing Every Day, That's The Way (I'm Only Trying To Help You).*
B. *Church Of The Poison Mind, Miss Me Blind, Mr. Man, Stormkeeper, Victims.*

The Boy George File:

Full name: George Alan O'Dowd.
Date of birth: June 14, 1961.
Height: 5 feet 11 inches.
Weight: 154 pounds.
Family home: Woolwich, south-east London.
George's address: No fixed abode. He is always
    moving around.
School: Eltham Green, London.
Exams passed: None.
First public performance: Bow Wow Wow show at the
    London Rainbow, 1981.
Early influence: David Bowie.
First Culture Club performance: Crocs, Rayleigh,
    Essex, October 1981.
First single released: White Bay May 21, 1982.
Favorite food: Japanese and Indian.
Favorite drink: Water; pernod and blackcurrant.
Likes: Being in love.
Hates: Rock journalists. Crowds.
Personal influence: Jon Moss, Culture Club's drummer.
Favorite color: George likes every color.
Favorite groups: Madness, Musical Youth.
Favorite singers: Ella Fitzgerald, Dolly Parton,
    Cliff Richard, Michael Jackson, Gladys Knight,
    Tom Jones.
*Favorite books: Ten Little Niggers, The Hobbit, Alice
    in Wonderland.*
Favorite records: Melting Pot ... Blue Mink
    Not Unusual ... Tom Jones
    24 Hours From Tulsa ... Gene Pitney
    Jolene ... Dolly Parton
    The Way We Were ... Gladys Knight and the Pips.
*Favorite films: Quest For Fire, The Sound Of Music,
    Great Expectations, Chitty Chitty Bang Bang,
    101 Dalmatians.*
Ideal night out: Relaxing in a good restaurant with
    close friends.

Picture acknowledgements:
J. Fraser/Impact
London Features International
Brian Moody/Sunday/Colorific
Pictorial Press
Barry Plummer
David Redfern
Rex Features
Frank Spooner/Gamma
Syndication International
Virgin Records
Chris Walter/Photofeatures

Multimedia Publications (UK) Limited have
endeavored to observe the legal requirements
with regard to the rights of the suppliers of graphic
and photographic materials.